I0820070

Wild about dads.

PHILIP BUNTING

It's not only humans who can be great dads. There are plenty of fantastic fathers out in the wild, too! Many wild dads go to great lengths to give their children the best chance of growing up healthy, smart and strong.

Some dads show their kids the ropes.

Gorilla.

Gorilla dads make great role models for their children. As baby gorillas grow, their father teaches them how to find food, how to play and how to look after one another. A gorilla dad takes pride in setting a good example for his little ones, and they form strong, loving bonds by doing so.

Some dads have a long commute.

Sandgrouse.

These desert-dwelling dads fly great distances to fetch water for their hatchlings. Once he finds fresh water, a father sandgrouse soaks his feathers, picking up as much water as he possibly can, and carries it back to the nest for his chicks and grouse spouse to drink.

Some dads keep their babies close.

Seahorse.

Once a mother seahorse lays her eggs, the fishy father-to-be incubates the eggs in a special pouch on his belly for the best part of a month. The tiny seahorse babies will emerge from the pouch as soon as they are ready to make their way into the big blue.

Some dads teach their young to hunt.

Arctic fox.

As arctic fox pups grow up, father fox plays a leading role in teaching them to be, well, foxy! He shows them how to hunt, to play, to hide and to flourish. Arctic fox dads are great providers and protectors, nurturing their pups until they're ready to go their own way.

Some dads carry a heavy load.

Giant water bug.
Some female water bugs lay their eggs on top of the dad-to-be's buggy back, not stopping until it is completely covered! Daddy bug then carries the eggs around with him for a few weeks – taking great care to keep them safe and clean – until, one by one, the eggs begin to hatch and dad can take a well-earned breather. Phew!

Some dads serve up a barfy breakfast.

Flamingo.

Flamingo fathers make excellent carers from the very beginning, taking turns with the mother to incubate and turn their eggs. When the baby flamingos hatch, both parents will take turns to feed them crop milk – a regurgitated secretion stewed up from what mom and dad ate the night before. And you thought your dad's cooking was questionable ...

Some dads can be a bit protective.

Australian magpie.
During the spring – when his babies are in the nest – an Australian magpie dad defends his young by swooping at anything he thinks could be a threat, including innocent passers-by. Ouch!

Some dads take their kids out to lunch.

Swan.

Swan dads take turns with their partner to incubate their eggs until they hatch. Once the cygnets (that's a fancy word for baby swans) hatch, they often hitch a ride on dad's shoulders while he hunts for their lunch.

Some dads find their kids a home.

Blue poison dart frog.

Dart frogs' eggs need to stay wet to survive. However, their forest home is not always damp enough for them. So, to keep his eggs from drying out while he waits for them to hatch into tadpoles, the father frog regularly pees on them! Once the tadpoles have hatched, he carefully carries each one to its own little pool of fresh water, where it will become a froglet.

Wee!
Yep, that's the smell.

Some dads bring home the groceries.

Great horned owl.

These dads take pride in delivering food to their families. At the top of this feathered father's shopping list are tasty treats such as mice, rabbits, lizards and frogs. Sounds delicious, right?

Not all dads are perfect.*

Grizzly bear.

Hungry grizzly fathers have been known to, well, how do I say this ... make a meal of their own cubs. No wonder they call them grizzly.

*No dad is perfect! Not even the really good ones.

Some dads have quite fishy breath.

Hardhead catfish.
These saltwater dads carry their eggs around in their mouths until the baby catfish are ready to swim free. During this time, the doting daddy-to-be will go without a single bite to eat. Just be careful not to swallow those babies in the meantime, Mr Catfish!

Some dads attract an unruly mob.

Emu.

Emu dads sit on the nest for almost two months without a break! When the baby emus have hatched, the emu dad continues to take care of them – and often the chicks of other emus at the same time. In fact, emu fathers have been known to take care of forty chicks at once!

Some dads give piggybacks all day long.

Cotton-top tamarin.

Tamarins typically have two or three babies at a time. Once the baby monkeys are a few weeks old, daddy tamarin takes the lead in carrying them around. He carries the infants on his back all day, every day, handing them back to mom only when it's time to nurse. Once the babies are about a month old, they can eat soft food. At this point, dad takes on the dual role of Principal Piggybacker and Chief Banana-Masher.

Some dads adopt a baby in need.

Chinstrap penguin.

Same-sex partnerships are pretty common out in the wild. Male chinstrap penguins have been known to partner together to incubate and care for abandoned eggs, which hatch without a hitch!

Some dads nuture the strength of the pack.

Wolf.
Wolves work together to help raise their pups, with the daddy wolf taking the lead in guarding the den and hunting for food. Wolf fathers are very caring and nurture their pups until they are ready to run with the pack.

What does your dad do for you?

Grrr!

FOR MY BROTHER
MICHAEL

**These wild dads don't tell their children how to live.
They set an example for their children to follow.**

(Except for that grizzly bear, who has most likely made his final appearance in a book about parenting.)

Little Hare
an imprint of Hardie Grant Children's Publishing
Wurundjeri Country
Level 11, 36 Wellington Street
Collingwood Victoria 3066
Melbourne | Sydney | San Francisco

hardiegrant.com/childrens

ISBN: 9781761217029

First published in Australia in 2020
This edition published in 2026

Printed and bound in HeShan China, November 2025
by LEO Paper Products LTD.

The paper this book is printed on is from FSC® certified forests and other controlled sources. FSC® promotes environmentally responsible, socially beneficial and economically viable management of the world's forests.

5 4 3 2 1

Hardie Grant acknowledges the Traditional Owners of the Country on which we work, the Wurundjeri People of the Kulin Nation and the Gadigal People of the Eora Nation, and recognises their continuing connection to the land, waters and culture. We pay our respects to their Elders past and present.